One -Year

Bible Reading

Almanac

Edited by

Josef Kraus

January 1

Genesis 1, 2
Matthew 1

January 2

Genesis 3, 4, 5
Matthew 2

January 3

Genesis 6, 7, 8
Matthew 3

January 4

Genesis 9, 10, 11
Matthew 4

January 5

Genesis 12, 13, 14
Matthew 5:1-26

January 6

Genesis 15, 16, 17
Matthew 5:27-48

January 7

Genesis 18, 19
Matthew 6

January 8

Genesis 20, 21, 22
Matthew 7

January 9

Genesis 23, 24
Matthew 8

January 10

Genesis 25, 26
Matthew 9:1-17

January 11

Genesis 27, 28
Matthew 9:18-38

January 12

Genesis 29, 30
Matthew 10:1-23

January 13

Genesis 31, 32
Matthew 10:24-42

January 14

Genesis 33, 34, 35
Matthew 11

January 15

Genesis 36, 37
Matthew 12:1-21

January 16

Genesis 38, 39, 40
Matthew 12:22-50

January

January 17

Genesis 41
Matthew 13:1-32

January 18

Genesis 42, 43
Matthew 13:33-58

January 19

Genesis 44, 45
Matthew 14:1-21

January 20

Genesis 46, 47, 48
Matthew 14:22-36

January 21

Genesis 49, 50
Matthew 15:1-20

January 22

Exodus 1, 2, 3
Matthew 15:21-39

January 23

Exodus 4, 5, 6
Matthew 16

January 24

Exodus 7, 8
Matthew 17

January 25

Exodus 9, 10
Matthew 18:1-20

January 26

Exodus 11, 12
Matthew 18:21-35

January 27

Exodus 13, 14, 15
Matthew 19:1-15

January 28

Exodus 16, 17, 18
Matthew 19:16-30

January 29

Exodus 19, 20, 21
Matthew 20:1-16

January 30

Exodus 22, 23, 24
Matthew 20:17-34

January 31

Exodus 25, 26
Matthew 21:1-22

February 1

Exodus 27, 28
Matthew 21:23-46

February 2

Exodus 29, 30
Matthew 22:1-22

February 3

Exodus 31, 32, 33
Matthew 22:23-46

February 4

Exodus 34, 35, 36
Matthew 23:1-22

February 5

Exodus 37, 38
Matthew 23:23-39

February 6

Exodus 39, 40
Matthew 24:1-22

February 7

Leviticus 1, 2, 3
Matthew 24:23-51

February 8

Leviticus 4, 5, 6
Matthew 25:1-30

February 9

Leviticus 7, 8, 9
Matthew 25:31-46

February 10

Leviticus 10, 11, 12
Matthew 26:1-19

February 11

Leviticus 13
Matthew 26:20-54

February 12

Leviticus 14
Matthew 26:55-75

February 13

Leviticus 15, 16, 17
Matthew 27:1-31

February 14

Leviticus 18, 19
Matthew 27:32-66

February 15

Leviticus 20, 21
Matthew 28

February 16

Leviticus 22, 23
Mark 1:1-22

February

February 17

Leviticus 24, 25
Mark 1:23-45

February 18

Leviticus 26, 27
Mark 2

February 19

Numbers 1, 2
Mark 3:1-21

February 20

Numbers 3, 4
Mark 3:22-35

February 21

Numbers 5, 6
Mark 4:1-20

February 22

Numbers 7
Mark 4:21-41

February 23

Numbers 8, 9, 10
Mark 5:1-20

February 24

Numbers 11, 12, 13
Mark 5:21-43

February 25

Numbers 14, 15
Mark 6:1-32

February 26

Numbers 16, 17
Mark 6:33-56

February 27

Numbers 18, 19, 20
Mark 7:1-13

February 28

Numbers 21, 22
Mark 7:14-37

February 29

Numbers 23, 24, 25
Mark 8:1-21

March 1

Numbers 26, 27
Mark 8:22-38

March 2

Numbers 28, 29
Mark 9:1-29

March 3

Numbers 30, 31
Mark 9:30-50

March 4

Numbers 32, 33
Mark 10:1-31

March 5

Numbers 34, 35, 36
Mark 10:32-52

March 6

Deuteronomy 1, 2
Mark 11:1-19

March 7

Deuteronomy 3, 4
Mark 11:20-33

March 8

Deuteronomy 5, 6, 7
Mark 12:1-27

March 9

Deuteronomy 8, 9, 10
Mark 12:28-44

March 10

Deuteronomy 11, 12, 13
Mark 13:1-13

March 11

Deuteronomy 14, 15, 16
Mark 13:14-37

March 12

Deuteronomy 17, 18, 19
Mark 14:1-25

March 13

Deuteronomy 20, 21, 22
Mark 14:26-50

March 14

Deuteronomy 23, 24, 25
Mark 14:51-72

March 15

Deuteronomy 26, 27
Mark 15:1-26

March 16

Deuteronomy 28
Mark 15:27-47

March

March 17

Deuteronomy 29, 30
Mark 16

March 18

Deuteronomy 31, 32
Luke 1:1-23

March 19

Deuteronomy 33, 34
Luke 1:24-56

March 20

Joshua 1, 2, 3
Luke 1:57-80

March 21

Joshua 4, 5, 6
Luke 2:1-24

March 22

Joshua 7, 8
Luke 2:25-52

March 23

Joshua 9, 10
Luke 3

March 24

Joshua 11, 12, 13
Luke 4:1-32

March 25

Joshua 14, 15
Luke 4:33-44

March 26

Joshua 16, 17, 18
Luke 5:1-16

March 27

Joshua 19, 20
Luke 5:17-39

March 28

Joshua 21, 22
Luke 6:1-26

March 29

Joshua 23, 24
Luke 6:27-49

March 30

Judges 1, 2
Luke 7:1-30

March 31

Judges 3, 4, 5
Luke 7:31-50

April 1

Judges 6, 7
Luke 8:1-21

April 2

Judges 8, 9
Luke 8:22-56

April 3

Judges 10, 11
Luke 9:1-36

April 4

Judges 12, 13, 14
Luke 9:37-62

April 5

Judges 15, 16, 17
Luke 10:1-24

April 6

Judges 18, 19
Luke 10:25-42

April 7

Judges 20, 21
Luke 11:1-28

April 8

Ruth
Luke 11:29-54

April 9

1 Samuel 1, 2, 3
Luke 12:1-34

April 10

1 Samuel 4, 5, 6
Luke 12:35-59

April 11

1 Samuel 7, 8, 9
Luke 13:1-21

April 12

1 Samuel 10, 11, 12
Luke 13:22-35

April 13

1 Samuel 13, 14
Luke 14:1-24

April 14

1 Samuel 15, 16
Luke 14:25-35

April 15

1 Samuel 17, 18
Luke 15:1-10

April 16

1 Samuel 19, 20, 21
Luke 15:11-32

April

April 17

1 Samuel 22, 23, 24
Luke 16:1-18

April 18

1 Samuel 25, 26
Luke 16:19-31

April 19

1 Samuel 27, 28, 29
Luke 17:1-19

April 20

1 Samuel 30, 31
Luke 17:20-37

April 21

2 Samuel 1, 2, 3
Luke 18:1-17

April 22

2 Samuel 4, 5, 6
Luke 18:18-43

April 23

2 Samuel 7, 8, 9
Luke 19:1-28

April 24

2 Samuel 10, 11, 12
Luke 19:29-48

April 25

2 Samuel 13, 14
Luke 20:1-26

April 26

2 Samuel 15, 16
Luke 20:27-47

April 27

2 Samuel 17, 18
Luke 21:1-19

April 28

2 Samuel 19, 20
Luke 21:20-38

April 29

2 Samuel 21, 22
Luke 22:1-30

April 30

2 Samuel 23, 24
Luke 22:31-53

May 1

1 Kings 1, 2
Luke 22:54-71

May 2

1 Kings 3, 4, 5
Luke 23:1-26

May 3

1 Kings 6, 7
Luke 23:27-38

May 4

1 Kings 8, 9
Luke 23:39-56

May 5

1 Kings 10, 11
Luke 24:1-35

May 6

1 Kings 12, 13
Luke 24:36-53

May 7

1 Kings 14, 15
John 1:1-28

May 8

1 Kings 16, 17, 18
John 1:29-51

May 9

1 Kings 19, 20
John 2

May 10

1 Kings 21, 22
John 3:1-21

May 11

2 Kings 1, 2, 3
John 3:22-36

May 12

2 Kings 4, 5
John 4:1-30

May 13

2 Kings 6, 7, 8
John 4:31-54

May 14

2 Kings 9, 10, 11
John 5:1-24

May 15

2 Kings 12, 13, 14
John 5:25-47

May 16

2 Kings 15, 16, 17
John 6:1-21

May

May 17

2 Kings 18, 19
John 6:22-44

May 18

2 Kings 20, 21, 22
John 6:45-71

May 19

2 Kings 23, 24, 25
John 7:1-31

May 20

1 Chronicles 1, 2
John 7:32-53

May 21

1 Chronicles 3, 4, 5
John 8:1-20

May 22

1 Chronicles 6, 7
John 8:21-36

May 23

1 Chronicles 8, 9, 10
John 8:37-59

May 24

1 Chronicles 11, 12, 13
John 9:1-23

May 25

1 Chronicles 14, 15, 16
John 9:24-41

May 26

1 Chronicles 17, 18, 19
John 10:1-21

May 27

1 Chronicles 20, 21, 22
John 10:22-42

May 28

1 Chronicles 23, 24, 25
John 11:1-17

May 29

1 Chronicles 26, 27
John 11:18-46

May 30

1 Chronicles 28, 29
John 11:47-57

May 31

2 Chronicles 1, 2, 3
John 12:1-19

June 1

2 Chronicles 4, 5, 6
John 12:20-50

June 2

2 Chronicles 7, 8, 9
John 13:1-17

June 3

2 Chronicles 10, 11, 12
John 13:18-38

June 4

2 Chronicles 13-16
John 14

June 5

2 Chronicles 17, 18, 19
John 15

June 6

2 Chronicles 20, 21, 22
John 16:1-15

June 7

2 Chronicles 23, 24, 25
John 16:16-33

June 8

2 Chronicles 26, 27, 28
John 17

June 9

2 Chronicles 29, 30, 31
John 18:1-23

June 10

2 Chronicles 32, 33
John 18:24-40

June 11

2 Chronicles 34, 35, 36
John 19:1-22

June 12

Ezra 1, 2
John 19:23-42

June 13

Ezra 3, 4, 5
John 20

June 14

Ezra 6, 7, 8
John 21

June 15

Ezra 9, 10
Acts 1

June 16

Nehemiah 1, 2, 3
Acts 2:1-13

June

June 17

Nehemiah 4, 5, 6
Acts 2:14-47

June 18

Nehemiah 7, 8
Acts 3

June 19

Nehemiah 9, 10, 11
Acts 4:1-22

June 20

Nehemiah 12, 13
Acts 4:23-37

June 21

Esther 1, 2, 3
Acts 5:1-16

June 22

Esther 4, 5, 6
Acts 5:17-42

June 23

Esther 7-10
Acts 6

June 24

Job 1, 2, 3
Acts 7:1-19

June 25

Job 4, 5, 6
Acts 7:20-43

June 26

Job 7, 8, 9
Acts 7:44-60

June 27

Job 10, 11, 12
Acts 8:1-25

June 28

Job 13, 14, 15
Acts 8:26-40

June 29

Job 16, 17, 18
Acts 9:1-22

June 30

Job 19, 20
Acts 9:23-43

July 1

Job 21, 22
Acts 10:1-23

July 2

Job 23, 24, 25
Acts 10:24-48

July 3

Job 26, 27, 28
Acts 11

July 4

Job 29, 30
Acts 12

July 5

Job 31, 32
Acts 13:1-23

July 6

Job 33, 34
Acts 13:24-52

July 7

Job 35, 36, 37
Acts 14

July 8

Job 38, 39
Acts 15:1-21

July 9

Job 40, 41, 42
Acts 15:22-41

July 10

Psalm 1, 2, 3
Acts 16:1-15

July 11

Psalm 4, 5, 6
Acts 16:16-40

July 12

Psalm 7, 8, 9
Acts 17:1-15

July 13

Psalm 10, 11, 12
Acts 17:16-34

July 14

Psalm 13-16
Acts 18

July 15

Psalm 17, 18
Acts 19:1-20

July 16

Psalm 19, 20, 21
Acts 19:21-41

July

July 17

Psalm 22, 23, 24
Acts 20:1-16

July 18

Psalm 25, 26, 27
Acts 20:17-38

July 19

Psalm 28, 29, 30
Acts 21:1-14

July 20

Psalm 31, 32, 33
Acts 21:15-40

July 21

Psalm 34, 35
Acts 22

July 22

Psalm 36, 37
Acts 23:1-11

July 23

Psalm 38, 39, 40
Acts 23:12-35

July 24

Psalm 41, 42, 43
Acts 24

July 25

Psalm 44, 45, 46
Acts 25

July 26

Psalm 47, 48, 49
Acts 26

July 27

Psalm 50, 51, 52
Acts 27:1-25

July 28

Psalm 53, 54, 55
Acts 27:26-44

July 29

Psalm 56, 57, 58
Acts 28:1-15

July 30

Psalm 59, 60, 61
Acts 28:16-31

July 31

Psalm 62, 63, 64
Romans 1

August 1

Psalm 65, 66, 67
Romans 2

August 2

Psalm 68, 69
Romans 3

August 3

Psalm 70, 71, 72
Romans 4

August 4

Psalm 73, 74
Romans 5

August 5

Psalm 75, 76, 77
Romans 6

August 6

Psalm 78
Romans 7

August 7

Psalm 79, 80, 81
Romans 8:1-18

August 8

Psalm 82, 83, 84
Romans 8:19-39

August 9

Psalm 85, 86, 87
Romans 9

August 10

Psalm 88, 89
Romans 10

August 11

Psalm 90, 91, 92
Romans 11:1-21

August 12

Psalm 93, 94, 95
Romans 11:22-36

August 13

Psalm 96, 97, 98
Romans 12

August 14

Psalm 99-102
Romans 13

August 15

Psalm 103, 104
Romans 14

August 16

Psalm 105, 106
Romans 15:1-20

August

August 17

Psalm 107, 108
Romans 15:21-33

August 18

Psalm 109, 110, 111
Romans 16

August 19

Psalm 112-115
1 Corinthians 1

August 20

Psalm 116-118
1 Corinthians 2

August 21

Psalm 119:1-48
1 Corinthians 3

August 22

Psalm 119:49-104
1 Corinthians 4

August 23

Psalm 119:105-176
1 Corinthians 5

August 24

Psalm 120-123
1 Corinthians 6

August 25

Psalm 124-127
1 Corinthians 7:1-24

August 26

Psalm 128-131
1 Corinthians 7:25-40

August 27

Psalm 132-135
1 Corinthians 8

August 28

Psalm 136-138
1 Corinthians 9

August 29

Psalm 139-141
1 Corinthians 10:1-13

August 30

Psalm 142-144
1 Corinthians 10:14-33

August 31

Psalm 145-147
1 Corinthians 11:1-15

September 1

Psalm 148-150
1 Corinthians 11:16-34

September 2

Proverbs 1, 2
1 Corinthians 12

September 3

Proverbs 3, 4
1 Corinthians 13

September 4

Proverbs 5, 6
1 Corinthians 14:1-20

September 5

Proverbs 7, 8
1 Corinthians 14:21-40

September 6

Proverbs 9, 10
1 Corinthians 15:1-32

September 7

Proverbs 11, 12
1 Corinthians 15:33-58

September 8

Proverbs 13, 14
1 Corinthians 16

September 9

Proverbs 15, 16
2 Corinthians 1

September 10

Proverbs 17, 18
2 Corinthians 2

September 11

Proverbs 19, 20
2 Corinthians 3

September 12

Proverbs 21, 22
2 Corinthians 4

September 13

Proverbs 23, 24
2 Corinthians 5

September 14

Proverbs 25, 26, 27
2 Corinthians 6

September 15

Proverbs 28, 29
2 Corinthians 7

September 16

Proverbs 30, 31
2 Corinthians 8

September

September 17

Ecclesiastes 1, 2, 3
2 Corinthians 9

September 18

Ecclesiastes 4, 5, 6
2 Corinthians 10

September 19

Ecclesiastes 7, 8, 9
2 Corinthians 11:1-15

September 20

Ecclesiastes 10, 11, 12
2 Corinthians 11:16-33

September 21

Song of Solomon 1, 2, 3
2 Corinthians 12

September 22

Song of Solomon 4, 5
2 Corinthians 13

September 23

Song of Solomon 6, 7, 8
Galatians 1

September 24

Isaiah 1, 2, 3
Galatians 2

September 25

Isaiah 4, 5, 6
Galatians 3

September 26

Isaiah 7, 8, 9
Galatians 4

September 27

Isaiah 10, 11, 12
Galatians 5

September 28

Isaiah 13, 14, 15
Galatians 6

September 29

Isaiah 16, 17, 18
Ephesians 1

September 30

Isaiah 19, 20, 21
Ephesians 2

October 1

Isaiah 22, 23
Ephesians 3

October 2

Isaiah 24, 25, 26
Ephesians 4

October 3

Isaiah 27, 28
Ephesians 5

October 4

Isaiah 29, 30
Ephesians 6

October 5

Isaiah 31, 32, 33
Philippians 1

October 6

Isaiah 34, 35, 36
Philippians 2

October 7

Isaiah 37, 38
Philippians 3

October 8

Isaiah 39, 40
Philippians 4

October 9

Isaiah 41, 42
Colossians 1

October 10

Isaiah 43, 44
Colossians 2

October 11

Isaiah 45, 46, 47
Colossians 3

October 12

Isaiah 48, 49
Colossians 4

October 13

Isaiah 50, 51, 52
1 Thessalonians 1

October 14

Isaiah 53, 54, 55
1 Thessalonians 2

October 15

Isaiah 56, 57, 58
1 Thessalonians 3

October 16

Isaiah 59, 60, 61
1 Thessalonians 4

October

October 17

Isaiah 62, 63, 64
1 Thessalonians 5

October 18

Isaiah 65, 66
2 Thessalonians 1

October 19

Jeremiah 1, 2
2 Thessalonians 2

October 20

Jeremiah 3, 4
2 Thessalonians 3

October 21

Jeremiah 5, 6
1 Timothy 1

October 22

Jeremiah 7, 8
1 Timothy 2

October 23

Jeremiah 9, 10
1 Timothy 3

October 24

Jeremiah 11, 12, 13
1 Timothy 4

October 25

Jeremiah 14, 15, 16
1 Timothy 5

October 26

Jeremiah 17, 18, 19
1 Timothy 6

October 27

Jeremiah 20, 21, 22
2 Timothy 1

October 28

Jeremiah 23, 24
2 Timothy 2

October 29

Jeremiah 25, 26
2 Timothy 3

October 30

Jeremiah 27, 28
2 Timothy 4

October 31

Jeremiah 29, 30
Titus 1

November 1

Jeremiah 31, 32
Titus 2

November 2

Jeremiah 33, 34, 35
Titus 3

November 3

Jeremiah 36, 37
Philemon

November 4

Jeremiah 38, 39
Hebrews 1

November 5

Jeremiah 40, 41, 42
Hebrews 2

November 6

Jeremiah 43, 44, 45
Hebrews 3

November 7

Jeremiah 46, 47, 48
Hebrews 4

November 8

Jeremiah 49, 50
Hebrews 5

November 9

Jeremiah 51, 52
Hebrews 6

November 10

Lamentations 1, 2
Hebrews 7

November 11

Lamentations 3, 4, 5
Hebrews 8

November 12

Ezekiel 1, 2, 3
Hebrews 9

November 13

Ezekiel 4, 5, 6
Hebrews 10:1-23

November 14

Ezekiel 7, 8, 9
Hebrews 10:24-39

November 15

Ezekiel 10, 11, 12
Hebrews 11:1-19

November 16

Ezekiel 13, 14, 15
Hebrews 11:20-40

November

November 17

Ezekiel 16
Hebrews 12

November 18

Ezekiel 17, 18, 19
Hebrews 13

November 19

Ezekiel 20, 21
James 1

November 20

Ezekiel 22, 23
James 2

November 21

Ezekiel 24, 25, 26
James 3

November 22

Ezekiel 27, 28
James 4

November 23

Ezekiel 29, 30, 31
James 5

November 24

Ezekiel 32, 33
1 Peter 1

November 25

Ezekiel 34, 35
1 Peter 2

November 26

Ezekiel 36, 37
1 Peter 3

November 27

Ezekiel 38, 39
1 Peter 4

November 28

Ezekiel 40
1 Peter 5

November 29

Ezekiel 41, 42
2 Peter 1

November 30

Ezekiel 43, 44
2 Peter 2

December 1

Ezekiel 45, 46
2 Peter 3

December 2

Ezekiel 47, 48
1 John 1

December 3

Daniel 1, 2
1 John 2

December 4

Daniel 3, 4
1 John 3

December 5

Daniel 5, 6
1 John 4

December 6

Daniel 7, 8
1 John 5

December 7

Daniel 9, 10
2 John

December 8

Daniel 11, 12
3 John

December 9

Hosea 1-4
Jude

December 10

Hosea 5-8
Revelation 1

December 11

Hosea 9, 10, 11
Revelation 2

December 12

Hosea 12, 13, 14
Revelation 3

December 13

Joel
Revelation 4

December 14

Amos 1, 2, 3
Revelation 5

December 15

Amos 4, 5, 6
Revelation 6

December 16

Amos 7, 8, 9
Revelation 7

December

December 17

Obadiah
Revelation 8

December 18

Jonah
Revelation 9

December 19

Micah 1, 2, 3
Revelation 10

December 20

Micah 4, 5
Revelation 11

December 21

Micah 6, 7
Revelation 12

December 22

Nahum
Revelation 13

December 23

Habakkuk
Revelation 14

December 24

Zephaniah
Revelation 15

December 25

Haggai
Revelation 16

December 26

Zechariah 1, 2, 3
Revelation 17

December 27

Zechariah 4, 5, 6
Revelation 18

December 28

Zechariah 7, 8, 9
Revelation 19

December 29

Zechariah 10, 11, 12
Revelation 20

December 30

Zechariah 13, 14
Revelation 21

December 31

Malachi
Revelation 22

Old Testament

Genesis

(1)1:1 (2)2:1 (3)3:1 (4)4:1
(5)5:1 (6)6:1 (7)7:1 (8)8:1
(9)9:1 (10)10:1 (11)11:1
(12)12:1 (13)13:1 (14)14:1
(15)15:1 (16)16:1 (17)17:1
(18)18:1 (19)19:1 (20)20:1
(21)21:1 (22)22:1 (23)23:1
(24)24:1 (25)25:1 (26)26:1
(27)27:1 (28)28:1 (29)29:1
(30)30:1 (31)31:1 (32)32:1
(33)33:1 (34)34:1 (35)35:1
(36)36:1 (37)37:1 (38)38:1
(39)39:1 (40)40:1 (41)41:1
(42)42:1 (43)43:1 (44)44:1
(45)45:1 (46)46:1 (47)47:1
(48)48:1 (49)49:1 (50)50:1

Exodus

(51)1:1 (52)2:1 (53)3:1 (54)4:1
(55)5:1 (56)6:1 (57)7:1 (58)8:1
(59)9:1 (60)10:1 (61)11:1
(62)12:1 (63)13:1 (64)14:1
(65)15:1 (66)16:1 (67)17:1
(68)18:1 (69)19:1 (70)20:1
(71)21:1 (72)22:1 (73)23:1
(74)24:1 (75)25:1 (76)26:1
(77)27:1 (78)28:1 (79)29:1
(80)30:1 (81)31:1 (82)32:1
(83)33:1 (84)34:1 (85)35:1
(86)36:1 (87)37:1 (88)38:1
(89)39:1 (90)40:1

Leviticus

(91)1:1 (92)2:1 (93)3:1 (94)4:1
(95)5:1 (96)6:1 (97)7:1 (98)8:1
(99)9:1 (100)10:1 (101)11:1
(102)12:1 (103)13:1 (104)14:1
(105)15:1 (106)16:1 (107)17:1
(108)18:1 (109)19:1 (110)20:1
(111)21:1 (112)22:1 (113)23:1
(114)24:1 (115)25:1 (116)26:1
(117)27:1

Numbers

(118)1:1 (119)2:1 (120)3:1
(121)4:1 (122)5:1 (123)6:1
(124)7:1 (125)8:1 (126)9:1
(127)10:1 (128)11:1 (129)12:1
(130)13:1 (131)14:1 (132)15:1
(133)16:1 (134)17:1 (135)18:1
(136)19:1 (137)20:1 (138)21:1
(139)22:1 (140)23:1 (141)24:1
(142)25:1 (143)26:1 (144)27:1
(145)28:1 (146)29:1 (147)30:1
(148)31:1 (149)32:1 (150)33:1
(151)34:1 (152)35:1 (153)36:1

Deuteronomy

(154)1:1 (155)2:1 (156)3:1
(157)4:1 (158)5:1 (159)6:1
(160)7:1 (161)8:1 (162)9:1
(163)10:1 (164)11:1 (165)12:1
(166)13:1 (167)14:1 (168)15:1
(169)16:1 (170)17:1 (171)18:1
(172)19:1 (173)20:1 (174)21:1
(175)22:1 (176)23:1 (177)24:1
(178)25:1 (179)26:1 (180)27:1
(181)28:1 (182)29:1 (183)30:1

(184)31:1 (185)32:1 (186)33:1
(187)34:1

Joshua

(188)1:1 (189)2:1 (190)3:1
(191)4:1 (192)5:1 (193)6:1
(194)7:1 (195)8:1 (196)9:1
(197)10:1 (198)11:1 (199)12:1
(200)13:1 (201)14:1 (202)15:1
(203)16:1 (204)17:1 (205)18:1
(206)19:1 (207)20:1 (208)21:1
(209)22:1 (210)23:1 (211)24:1

Judges

(212)1:1 (213)2:1 (214)3:1
(215)4:1 (216)5:1 (217)6:1
(218)7:1 (219)8:1 (220)9:1
(221)10:1 (222)11:1 (223)12:1
(224)13:1 (225)14:1 (226)15:1
(227)16:1 (228)17:1 (229)18:1
(230)19:1 (231)20:1 (232)21:1

Ruth

(233)1:1

1 Samuel

(234)1:1 (235)2:1 (236)3:1
(237)4:1 (238)5:1 (239)6:1
(240)7:1 (241)8:1 (242)9:1
(243)10:1 (244)11:1 (245)12:1
(246)13:1 (247)14:1 (248)15:1
(249)16:1 (250)17:1 (251)18:1
(252)19:1 (253)20:1 (254)21:1
(255)22:1 (256)23:1 (257)24:1
(258)25:1 (259)26:1 (260)27:1

(261)28:1 (262)29:1 (263)30:1
(264)31:1

2 Samuel

(265)1:1 (266)2:1 (267)3:1
(268)4:1 (269)5:1 (270)6:1
(271)7:1 (272)8:1 (273)9:1
(274)10:1 (275)11:1 (276)12:1
(277)13:1 (278)14:1 (279)15:1
(280)16:1 (281)17:1 (282)18:1
(283)19:1 (284)20:1 (285)21:1
(286)22:1 (287)23:1 (288)24:1

1 Kings

(289)1:1 (290)2:1 (291)3:1
(292)4:1 (293)5:1 (294)6:1
(295)7:1 (296)8:1 (297)9:1
(298)10:1 (299)11:1 (300)12:1
(301)13:1 (302)14:1 (303)15:1
(304)16:1 (305)17:1 (306)18:1
(307)19:1 (308)20:1 (309)21:1
(310)22:1

2 Kings

(311)1:1 (312)2:1 (313)3:1
(314)4:1 (315)5:1 (316)6:1
(317)7:1 (318)8:1 (319)9:1
(320)10:1 (321)11:1 (322)12:1
(323)13:1 (324)14:1 (325)15:1
(326)16:1 (327)17:1 (328)18:1
(329)19:1 (330)20:1 (331)21:1
(332)22:1 (333)23:1 (334)24:1
(335)25:1

1 Chronicles

(336)1:1 (337)2:1 (338)3:1
(339)4:1 (340)5:1 (341)6:1
(342)7:1 (343)8:1 (344)9:1
(345)10:1 (346)11:1 (347)12:1
(348)13:1 (349)14:1 (350)15:1
(351)16:1 (352)17:1 (353)18:1
(354)19:1 (355)20:1 (356)21:1
(357)22:1 (358)23:1 (359)24:1
(360)25:1 (361)26:1 (362)27:1
(363)28:1 (364)29:1

2 Chronicles

(365)1:1 (366)2:1 (367)3:1
(368)4:1 (369)5:1 (370)6:1
(371)7:1 (372)8:1 (373)9:1
(374)10:1 (375)11:1 (376)12:1
(377)13 (378)17:1 (379)18:1
(380)19:1 (381)20:1 (382)21:1
(383)22:1 (384)23:1 (385)24:1
(386)25:1 (387)26:1 (388)27:1
(389)28:1 (390)29:1 (391)30:1
(392)31:1 (393)32:1 (394)33:1
(395)34:1 (396)35:1 (397)36:1

Ezra

(398)1:1 (399)2:1 (400)3:1
(401)4:1 (402)5:1 (403)6:1
(404)7:1 (405)8:1 (406)9:1
(407)10:1

Nehemiah

(408)1:1 (409)2:1 (410)3:1
(411)4:1 (412)5:1 (413)6:1
(414)7:1 (415)8:1 (416)9:1

(417)10:1 (418)11:1 (419)12:1
(420)13:1

Esther

(421)1:1 (422)2:1 (423)3:1
(424)4:1 (425)5:1 (426)6:1
(427)7:1

Job

(428)1:1 (429)2:1 (430)3:1
(431)4:1 (432)5:1 (433)6:1
(434)7:1 (435)8:1 (436)9:1
(437)10:1 (438)11:1 (439)12:1
(440)13:1 (441)14:1 (442)15:1
(443)16:1 (444)17:1 (445)18:1
(446)19:1 (447)20:1 (448)21:1
(449)22:1 (450)23:1 (451)24:1
(452)25:1 (453)26:1 (454)27:1
(455)28:1 (456)29:1 (457)30:1
(458)31:1 (459)32:1 (460)33:1
(461)34:1 (462)35:1 (463)36:1
(464)37:1 (465)38:1 (466)39:1
(467)40:1 (468)41:1 (469)42:1

Psalms

(470)1:1 (471)2:1 (472)3:1
(473)4:1 (474)5:1 (475)6:1
(476)7:1 (477)8:1 (478)9:1
(479)10:1 (480)11:1 (481)12:1
(482)13 (483)17:1 (484)18:1
(485)19:1 (486)20:1 (487)21:1
(488)22:1 (489)23:1 (490)24:1
(491)25:1 (492)26:1 (493)27:1
(494)28:1 (495)29:1 (496)30:1
(497)31:1 (498)32:1 (499)33:1
(500)34:1 (501)35:1 (502)36:1
(503)37:1 (504)38:1 (505)39:1

(506)40:1 (507)41:1 (508)42:1
(509)43:1 (510)44:1 (511)45:1
(512)46:1 (513)47:1 (514)48:1
(515)49:1 (516)50:1 (517)51:1
(518)52:1 (519)53:1 (520)54:1
(521)55:1 (522)56:1 (523)57:1
(524)58:1 (525)59:1 (526)60:1
(527)61:1 (528)62:1 (529)63:1
(530)64:1 (531)65:1 (532)66:1
(533)67:1 (534)68:1 (535)69:1
(536)70:1 (537)71:1 (538)72:1
(539)73:1 (540)74:1 (541)75:1
(542)76:1 (543)77:1 (544)78:1
(545)79:1 (546)80:1 (547)81:1
(548)82:1 (549)83:1 (550)84:1
(551)85:1 (552)86:1 (553)87:1
(554)88:1 (555)89:1 (556)90:1
(557)91:1 (558)92:1 (559)93:1
(560)94:1 (561)95:1 (562)96:1
(563)97:1 (564)98:1 (565)99
(566)103:1 (567)104:1
(568)105:1 (569)106:1
(570)107:1 (571)108:1
(572)109:1 (573)110:1
(574)111:1 (575)112:1
(576)116:1 (577)119:1-48
(578)119:49-104 (579)119:105-
176 (580)120:1 (581)124:1
(582)128:1 (583)132:1
(584)136:1 (585)139:1
(586)142:1 (587)145:1
(588)148:1

Proverbs

(589)1:1 (590)2:1 (591)3:1
(592)4:1 (593)5:1 (594)6:1
(595)7:1 (596)8:1 (597)9:1
(598)10:1 (599)11:1 (600)12:1
(601)13:1 (602)14:1 (603)15:1

(604)16:1 (605)17:1 (606)18:1
(607)19:1 (608)20:1 (609)21:1
(610)22:1 (611)23:1 (612)24:1
(613)25:1 (614)26:1 (615)27:1
(616)28:1 (617)29:1 (618)30:1
(619)31:1

Ecclesiastes

(620)1:1 (621)2:1 (622)3:1
(623)4:1 (624)5:1 (625)6:1
(626)7:1 (627)8:1 (628)9:1
(629)10:1 (630)11:1 (631)12:1

Song of Solomon

(632)1:1 (633)2:1 (634)3:1
(635)4:1 (636)5:1 (637)6:1
(638)7:1 (639)8:1

Isaiah

(640)1:1 (641)2:1 (642)3:1
(643)4:1 (644)5:1 (645)6:1
(646)7:1 (647)8:1 (648)9:1
(649)10:1 (650)11:1 (651)12:1
(652)13:1 (653)14:1 (654)15:1
(655)16:1 (656)17:1 (657)18:1
(658)19:1 (659)20:1 (660)21:1
(661)22:1 (662)23:1 (663)24:1
(664)25:1 (665)26:1 (666)27:1
(667)28:1 (668)29:1 (669)30:1
(670)31:1 (671)32:1 (672)33:1
(673)34:1 (674)35:1 (675)36:1
(676)37:1 (677)38:1 (678)39:1
(679)40:1 (680)41:1 (681)42:1
(682)43:1 (683)44:1 (684)45:1
(685)46:1 (686)47:1 (687)48:1
(688)49:1 (689)50:1 (690)51:1
(691)52:1 (692)53:1 (693)54:1

(694)55:1 (695)56:1 (696)57:1
(697)58:1 (698)59:1 (699)60:1
(700)61:1 (701)62:1 (702)63:1
(703)64:1 (704)65:1 (705)66:1

Jeremiah

(706)1:1 (707)2:1 (708)3:1
(709)4:1 (710)5:1 (711)6:1
(712)7:1 (713)8:1 (714)9:1
(715)10:1 (716)11:1 (717)12:1
(718)13:1 (719)14:1 (720)15:1
(721)16:1 (722)17:1 (723)18:1
(724)19:1 (725)20:1 (726)21:1
(727)22:1 (728)23:1 (729)24:1
(730)25:1 (731)26:1 (732)27:1
(733)28:1 (734)29:1 (735)30:1
(736)31:1 (737)32:1 (738)33:1
(739)34:1 (740)35:1 (741)36:1
(742)37:1 (743)38:1 (744)39:1
(745)40:1 (746)41:1 (747)42:1
(748)43:1 (749)44:1 (750)45:1
(751)46:1 (752)47:1 (753)48:1
(754)49:1 (755)50:1 (756)51:1
(757)52:1

Lamentations

(758)1:1 (759)2:1 (760)3:1
(761)4:1 (762)5:1

Ezekiel

(763)1:1 (764)2:1 (765)3:1
(766)4:1 (767)5:1 (768)6:1
(769)7:1 (770)8:1 (771)9:1
(772)10:1 (773)11:1 (774)12:1
(775)13:1 (776)14:1 (777)15:1
(778)16:1 (779)17:1 (780)18:1
(781)19:1 (782)20:1 (783)21:1

(784)22:1 (785)23:1 (786)24:1
(787)25:1 (788)26:1 (789)27:1
(790)28:1 (791)29:1 (792)30:1
(793)31:1 (794)32:1 (795)33:1
(796)34:1 (797)35:1 (798)36:1
(799)37:1 (800)38:1 (801)39:1
(802)40:1 (803)41:1 (804)42:1
(805)43:1 (806)44:1 (807)45:1
(808)46:1 (809)47:1 (810)48:1

Daniel

(811)1:1 (812)2:1 (813)3:1
(814)4:1 (815)5:1 (816)6:1
(817)7:1 (818)8:1 (819)9:1
(820)10:1 (821)11:1 (822)12:1

Hosea

(823)1:1 (824)5:1 (825)9:1
(826)10:1 (827)11:1 (828)12:1
(829)13:1 (830)14:1

Joel

(831)1:1

Amos

(832)1:1 (833)2:1 (834)3:1
(835)4:1 (836)5:1 (837)6:1
(838)7:1 (839)8:1 (840)9:1

Obadiah

(841)1:1

Jonah

(842)1:1

Micah

(843)1:1 (844)2:1 (845)3:1
(846)4:1 (847)5:1 (848)6:1
(849)7:1

Nahum

(850)1:1

Habakkuk

(851)1:1

Zephaniah

(852)1:1

Haggai

(853)1:1

Zechariah

(854)1:1 (855)2:1 (856)3:1
(857)4:1 (858)5:1 (859)6:1
(860)7:1 (861)8:1 (862)9:1
(863)10:1 (864)11:1 (865)12:1
(866)13:1 (867)14:1

Malachi

(868)1:1

New Testament

Matthew

(869)1:1 (870)2:1 (871)3:1
(872)4:1 (873)5:1-26
(874)5:27-48 (875)6:1 (876)7:1
(877)8:1 (878)9:1-17
(879)9:18-38 (880)10:1-23
(881)10:24-42 (882)11:1
(883)12:1-21 (884)12:22-50
(885)13:1-32 (886)13:33-58
(887)14:1-21 (888)14:22-36
(889)15:1-20 (890)15:21-39
(891)16:1 (892)17:1 (893)18:1-
20 (894)18:21-35 (895)19:1-15
(896)19:16-30 (897)20:1-16
(898)20:17-34 (899)21:1-22
(900)21:23-46 (901)22:1-22
(902)22:23-46 (903)23:1-22
(904)23:23-39 (905)24:1-22
(906)24:23-51 (907)25:1-30
(908)25:31-46 (909)26:1-19
(910)26:20-54 (911)26:55-75
(912)27:1-31 (913)27:32-66
(914)28:1

Mark

(915)1:1-22 (916)1:23-45
(917)2:1 (918)3:1-21 (919)3:22-
35 (920)4:1-20 (921)4:21-41
(922)5:1-20 (923)5:21-43
(924)6:1-32 (925)6:33-56
(926)7:1-13 (927)7:14-37
(928)8:1-21 (929)8:22-38
(930)9:1-29 (931)9:30-50
(932)10:1-31 (933)10:32-52
(934)11:1-19 (935)11:20-33

(936)12:1-27 (937)12:28-44
(938)13:1-13 (939)13:14-37
(940)14:1-25 (941)14:26-50
(942)14:51-72 (943)15:1-26
(944)15:27-47 (945)16:1

Luke

(946)1:1-23 (947)1:24-56
(948)1:57-80 (949)2:1-24
(950)2:25-52 (951)3:1 (952)4:1-
32 (953)4:33-44 (954)5:1-16
(955)5:17-39 (956)6:1-26
(957)6:27-49 (958)7:1-30
(959)7:31-50 (960)8:1-21
(961)8:22-56 (962)9:1-36
(963)9:37-62 (964)10:1-24
(965)10:25-42 (966)11:1-28
(967)11:29-54 (968)12:1-34
(969)12:35-59 (970)13:1-21
(971)13:22-35 (972)14:1-24
(973)14:25-35 (974)15:1-10
(975)15:11-32 (976)16:1-18
(977)16:19-31 (978)17:1-19
(979)17:20-37 (980)18:1-17
(981)18:18-43 (982)19:1-28
(983)19:29-48 (984)20:1-26
(985)20:27-47 (986)21:1-19
(987)21:20-38 (988)22:1-30
(989)22:31-53 (990)22:54-71
(991)23:1-26 (992)23:27-38
(993)23:39-56 (994)24:1-35
(995)24:36-53

John

(996)1:1-28 (997)1:29-51
(998)2:1 (999)3:1-21
(1000)3:22-36 (1001)4:1-30
(1002)4:31-54 (1003)5:1-24

(1004)5:25-47 (1005)6:1-21
(1006)6:22-44 (1007)6:45-71
(1008)7:1-31 (1009)7:32-53
(1010)8:1-20 (1011)8:21-36
(1012)8:37-59 (1013)9:1-23
(1014)9:24-41 (1015)10:1-21
(1016)10:22-42 (1017)11:1-17
(1018)11:18-46 (1019)11:47-57
(1020)12:1-19 (1021)12:20-50
(1022)13:1-17 (1023)13:18-38
(1024)14:1 (1025)15:1
(1026)16:1-15 (1027)16:16-33
(1028)17:1 (1029)18:1-23
(1030)18:24-40 (1031)19:1-22
(1032)19:23-42 (1033)20:1
(1034)21:1

Acts

(1035)1:1 (1036)2:1-13
(1037)2:14-47 (1038)3:1
(1039)4:1-22 (1040)4:23-37
(1041)5:1-16 (1042)5:17-42
(1043)6:1 (1044)7:1-19
(1045)7:20-43 (1046)7:44-60
(1047)8:1-25 (1048)8:26-40
(1049)9:1-22 (1050)9:23-43
(1051)10:1-23 (1052)10:24-48
(1053)11:1 (1054)12:1
(1055)13:1-23 (1056)13:24-52
(1057)14:1 (1058)15:1-21
(1059)15:22-41 (1060)16:1-15
(1061)16:16-40 (1062)17:1-15
(1063)17:16-34 (1064)18:1
(1065)19:1-20 (1066)19:21-41
(1067)20:1-16 (1068)20:17-38
(1069)21:1-14 (1070)21:15-40
(1071)22:1 (1072)23:1-11
(1073)23:12-35 (1074)24:1
(1075)25:1 (1076)26:1

(1077)27:1-25 (1078)27:26-44
(1079)28:1-15 (1080)28:16-31

Romans

(1081)1:1 (1082)2:1 (1083)3:1
(1084)4:1 (1085)5:1 (1086)6:1
(1087)7:1 (1088)8:1-18
(1089)8:19-39 (1090)9:1
(1091)10:1 (1092)11:1-21
(1093)11:22-36 (1094)12:1
(1095)13:1 (1096)14:1
(1097)15:1-20 (1098)15:21-33
(1099)16:1

1 Corinthians

(1100)1:1 (1101)2:1 (1102)3:1
(1103)4:1 (1104)5:1 (1105)6:1
(1106)7:1-24 (1107)7:25-40
(1108)8:1 (1109)9:1
(1110)10:1-13 (1111)10:14-33
(1112)11:1-15 (1113)11:16-34
(1114)12:1 (1115)13:1
(1116)14:1-20 (1117)14:21-40
(1118)15:1-32 (1119)15:33-58
(1120)16:1

2 Corinthians

(1121)1:1 (1122)2:1 (1123)3:1
(1124)4:1 (1125)5:1 (1126)6:1
(1127)7:1 (1128)8:1 (1129)9:1
(1130)10:1 (1131)11:1-15
(1132)11:16-33 (1133)12:1
(1134)13:1

Galatians

(1135)1:1 (1136)2:1 (1137)3:1
(1138)4:1 (1139)5:1 (1140)6:1

Ephesians

(1141)1:1 (1142)2:1 (1143)3:1
(1144)4:1 (1145)5:1 (1146)6:1

Philippians

(1147)1:1 (1148)2:1 (1149)3:1
(1150)4:1

Colossians

(1151)1:1 (1152)2:1 (1153)3:1
(1154)4:1

1 Thessalonians

(1155)1:1 (1156)2:1 (1157)3:1
(1158)4:1 (1159)5:1

2 Thessalonians

(1160)1:1 (1161)2:1 (1162)3:1

1 Timothy

(1163)1:1 (1164)2:1 (1165)3:1
(1166)4:1 (1167)5:1 (1168)6:1

2 Timothy

(1169)1:1 (1170)2:1 (1171)3:1
(1172)4:1

Titus

(1173)1:1 (1174)2:1 (1175)3:1

Philemon

(1176)1:1

Hebrews

(1177)1:1 (1178)2:1 (1179)3:1
(1180)4:1 (1181)5:1 (1182)6:1
(1183)7:1 (1184)8:1 (1185)9:1
(1186)10:1-23 (1187)10:24-39
(1188)11:1-19 (1189)11:20-40
(1190)12:1 (1191)13:1

James

(1192)1:1 (1193)2:1 (1194)3:1
(1195)4:1 (1196)5:1

1 Peter

(1197)1:1 (1198)2:1 (1199)3:1
(1200)4:1 (1201)5:1

2 Peter

(1202)1:1 (1203)2:1 (1204)3:1

1 John

(1205)1:1 (1206)2:1 (1207)3:1
(1208)4:1 (1209)5:1

2 John

(1210)1:1

3 John

(1211)1:1

Jude

(1212)1:1

Revelation

(1213)1:1 (1214)2:1 (1215)3:1
(1216)4:1 (1217)5:1 (1218)6:1
(1219)7:1 (1220)8:1 (1221)9:1
(1222)10:1 (1223)11:1
(1224)12:1 (1225)13:1
(1226)14:1 (1227)15:1
(1228)16:1 (1229)17:1
(1230)18:1 (1231)19:1
(1232)20:1 (1233)21:1
(1234)22:1